M000189621

This Journal
Belongs to: